U.S. SEISMIC ZONES

THE HAWAIIAN ARCHIPELAGO

DANIELLE HAYNES

PowerKiDS press

Published in 2026 by The Rosen Publishing Group, Inc.
2544 Clinton Street, Buffalo, NY 14224

First Edition

Editor: Danielle Haynes
Book Design: Michael Flynn

Photo Credits: Cover MNStudio/Shutterstock.com; (series background) Picksell/Shutterstock.com; p. 4 zelvan/Shutterstock.com; p. 5 Omer Faruk/Shutterstock.com; p. 7 Robert Harding Video/Shutterstock.com; p. 9 https://commons.wikimedia.org/wiki/File:John_Tuzo_Wilson_in_1992.jpg; p. 11 https://commons.wikimedia.org/wiki/File:Hawaii_hotspot_cross-sectional_diagram.jpg; p. 13 Michail_Vorobyev/Shutterstock.com; p. 14 OUESTUSA/Shutterstock.com; p. 15 LanaG/Shutterstock.com; p. 17 NPS Photo; p. 18 Yvonne Baur/Shutterstock.com; p. 19 Dudarev Mikhail/Shutterstock.com; p. 20 Sierra Juliet/Shutterstock.com; p. 21 samoila ionut/Shutterstock.com; p. 22 Intrepix/Shutterstock.com; p. 23 https://commons.wikimedia.org/wiki/File:Waiohinu_Church_destroyed_by_the_earthquake,_1868,_photograph_by_H._L._Chase,_Mission_Houses_Museum_Archives_(variant).jpg; p. 24 Erlantz P.R/Shutterstock.com; p. 25 https://commons.wikimedia.org/wiki/File:Tsunami_large.jpg; p. 27 courtesy of USGS; p. 29 Michael Vi/Shutterstock.com.

Cataloging-in-Publication Data

Names: Haynes, Danielle.
Title: The Hawaiian Archipelago / Danielle Haynes.
Description: Buffalo, New York : PowerKids Press, 2026. | Series: U.S. seismic zones | Includes glossary and index.
Identifiers: ISBN 9781499453324 (pbk.) | ISBN 9781499453331 (library bound) | ISBN 9781499453348 (ebook)
Subjects: LCSH: Plate tectonics--Juvenile literature. | Earthquakes--Juvenile literature. | Volcanoes--Juvenile literature. | Seismology--Juvenile literature.
Classification: LCC QE511.4 H38 2026 | DDC 551.1'36--dc23

Manufactured in the United States of America

CPSIA Compliance Information: Batch #CSPK26. For further information contact Rosen Publishing at 1-800-237-9932.

CONTENTS

WELCOME TO THE HAWAIIAN ISLANDS

The Hawaiian Archipelago is a chain of 137 islands and smaller landmasses called islets, atolls, and shoals that stretches about 1,500 miles (2,400 km) in the North Pacific Ocean. Most people, however, know Hawaii for its eight largest islands: Hawaii, Maui, Kahoolawe, Lanai, Molokai, Oahu, Kauai, and Niihau.

Hawaii became the 50th and most recent U.S. state on August 21, 1959. It's about 2,397 miles (8,516 km) away from the mainland United States.

Hawaii's tropical locale and many beautiful beaches make it a popular vacation spot for people from the U.S. mainland.

Geologically, Hawaii is unlike any other state in the United States. For one thing, it's the only state that's not part of the North American continent. As islands, they don't belong to any of the Earth's continents. Also, unlike the rest of the United States, Hawaii sits on the Pacific tectonic plate. The rest of the United States is on the North American plate.

EARTH-SHAKING FACT!

Before becoming part of the United States, Hawaii was its own country ruled by a monarchy. Its last ruler was Queen Lili'uokalani.

WHAT IS AN ARCHIPELAGO?

The Hawaiian islands are what's known as an archipelago. This is a group or chain of islands, usually in the ocean, but also found in lakes and rivers. The word archipelago comes from the Italian word *archi* (chief or principal) and the Greek word *pelagus* (pool or pond).

The Hawaiian Archipelago—like most archipelagos—was formed by a chain of volcanoes under the sea erupting and building up the landmass above the ocean. An archipelago made up of ocean islands is also known as an island arc. Other archipelagos are formed from sediment that builds up on coral reefs. Some are even made by pieces of land breaking off from a larger, continental landmass.

EARTH-SHAKING FACT!

There are many seamounts associated with the Hawaiian archipelago. These are volcanoes—usually dormant—that haven't yet broken above the surface of the sea.

The Hawaiian Archipelago is made up of more than just the eight main islands most people know. There are dozens of islands, many not **inhabited**.

THE HAWAIIAN HOTSPOT

So how did the volcanoes that created the Hawaiian Archipelago form? Most volcanoes form where two tectonic plates meet. These plates are constantly moving—it's so slow you usually don't notice it unless an earthquake happens. Volcanoes form when these plates either come together or move apart. When this happens, **magma** from below the Earth's crust comes up between the plates and forms a volcano.

But that's not how it works in Hawaii. Remember, this archipelago sits in the middle of the Pacific plate. Plate tectonics do play a role in how Hawaii's volcanoes formed, but not in the typical way. These volcanoes were formed by what's known as a hotspot, a geologic formation first proposed by Canadian scientist J. Tuzo Wilson in 1963.

J. Tuzo Wilson served in the Canadian military during World War II, taught geophysics at the University of Toronto, and served as president of multiple scientific organizations.

J. TUZO WILSON

Canadian **geophysicist** J. Tuzo Wilson was very important to the study of plate tectonics. Scientists used to believe the Earth's plates were fixed in place. Wilson, though, renewed the theory of continental drift, or the idea that the plates move.

Most importantly concerning Hawaii, Wilson was the first person to explain how volcanic hotspots work. His work was so important, the Wilson mountain range in Antarctica was named after him!

Hotspots are also known as mantle thermal plumes. "Mantle" refers to the middle layer of the Earth, "thermal" means heated, and "plume" is the column of magma rising from the mantle to the Earth's surface.

This plume, or hotspot, is stationary. It doesn't move, but the Pacific plate above it does. The plume creates a volcano that eventually rises above the sea and forms an island. As the tectonic plate moves, though, that volcano moves away from the hotspot and becomes dormant. A new volcano forms. This is why the northwestern Hawaiian Islands are older and more eroded than the young ones to the southeast.

Scientists believe the Hawaiian hotspot has been releasing **lava** for about 70 million years, creating both the islands we see above the sea as well as the seamounts below.

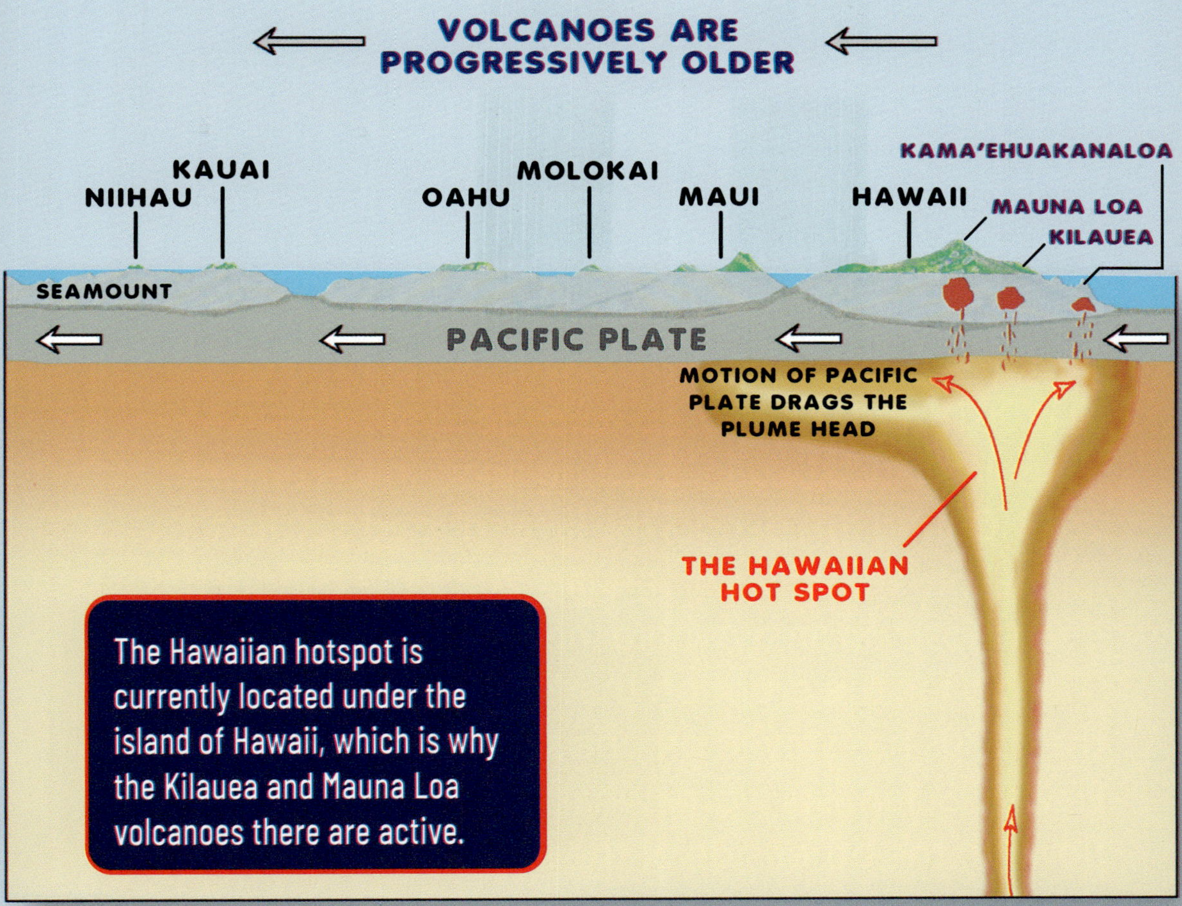

The Hawaiian hotspot is currently located under the island of Hawaii, which is why the Kilauea and Mauna Loa volcanoes there are active.

PELE, THE HAWAIIAN FIRE GODDESS

Even before scientists understood how plate tectonics worked, the Native Hawaiian people saw that the islands in the north were older than the ones in the south. They had a legend to explain this.

In Hawaiian **culture**, Pele is the goddess of fire and volcanoes who originally lived on the northern island of Kauai. Pele's sister, the sea goddess Namakaokahai, attacked her, forcing her to flee one by one to the more southern islands. Pele brought fire and volcanic activity with her each time she moved!

KILAUEA VOLCANO

Kilauea is the world's most active volcanic mass. It's a shield volcano, which are large with gentle slopes. Kilauea erupted off and on for more than three decades up until about 2018. Over several days in May 2018, the lava caused damage to more than 650 houses! Kilauea began erupting again in December 2024. During this period, the lava spurted 100 feet (30 m) into the air! As of January 2025, the danger has been mostly in areas where there are no homes.

So far, the eruption that's been ongoing since the 1980s has stayed on one side of the island of Hawaii. Scientists worry what will happen if the lava flows to the other side of the island like it has in the distant past.

CHRISTINA HELIKER

One scientist has spent more than 20 years studying Kilauea and its surrounding landscape—Christina Heliker. She is a geologist and volcanologist who started working at the site when the volcano began its latest eruption in 1983. While working with the Hawaiian Volcano **Observatory** (HVO), she took and studied samples of burning hot lava, helped teach locals about dangers, and even rescued pets abandoned during evacuations. She wrote the book *Kilauea: The Newest Land on Earth* in 1999.

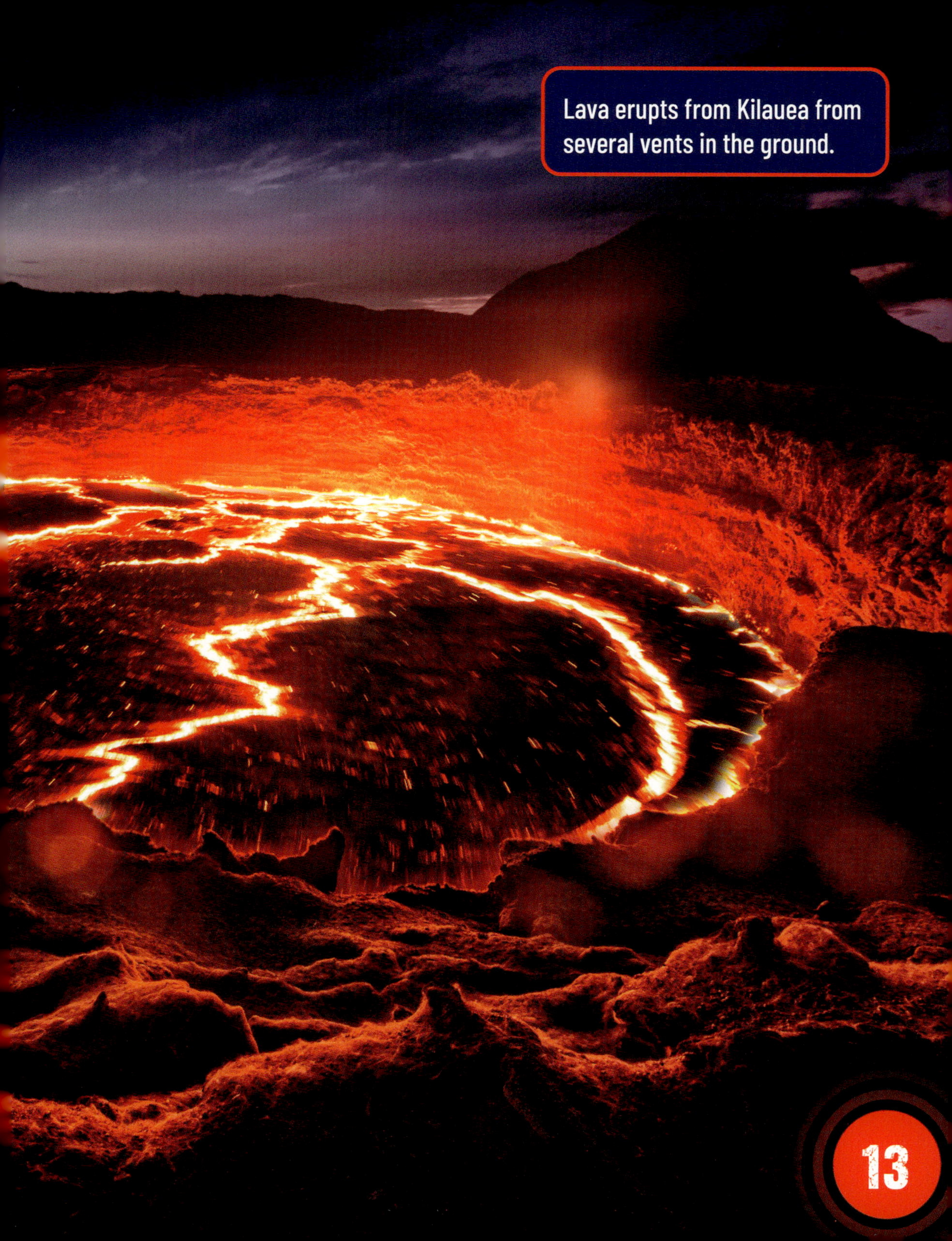

Lava erupts from Kilauea from several vents in the ground.

PELE'S HAIR

Even if a person doesn't go anywhere near an active volcano's hot lava, it can still be very dangerous for them. Gas bubbles can cause the hot lava to stretch out into thin strands that then go **airborne**. These strands are like thin glass fibers. Locals call this Pele's hair. Because it's basically glass, it's very dangerous to breathe it in or get on your skin or in your eyes. The strands will often gather in low-lying areas many inches deep.

Pele's hair gathers on the ground near a volcanic eruption.

EARTH-SHAKING FACT!

Birds have even made nests out of Pele's hair!

Breathing volcanic gases is dangerous for humans.

Volcanoes also **emit** toxic gases such as sulfur dioxide. This combines with the Earth's atmosphere to create a haziness scientists call vog, or volcanic fog. Vog can cause problems for people with breathing troubles or other health issues. It can also **irritate** the eyes, nose, throat, and skin.

HAWAII VOLCANOES NATIONAL PARK

Did you know you can hike along the edge of an active volcano crater in Hawaii? That may sound wild, but that's just what you can do at Hawaii Volcanoes National Park on the Big Island. The volcanoes Kilauea and Mauna Loa are the highlights of the park, which is operated by the U.S. government.

The area has long been an important cultural site for Native Hawaiians. Today's scientists also value the geological importance of the site. That's why the government decided to protect it in 1916 by designating it a national park. The United Nations also named the volcanoes here a World **Heritage** Site, meaning they'll be well protected for future generations. Visitors can hike, take scenic drives, and learn more about volcanoes through special programs.

EARTH-SHAKING FACT!

During times when Kilauea is active, the U.S. Geological Survey makes a live stream available to the public on its YouTube page.

Park archaeologist Summer Roper Todd stands on a dried lava flow in Hawaii Volcanoes National Park.

GROWING ISLANDS

Growing a new island from a volcano takes millions of years. It's a slow process, but with the Hawaiian hotspot, we can see many steps of the process in action today. We can see the above-ground growth of Kilauea and Mauna Loa on the island of Hawaii—also called the Big Island. We can see the now-eroded dormant volcanoes in the more northern islands.

And if you look underwater southeast of the Big Island, you can see the early stages of a seamount that will eventually become a new island. Kama'ehuakanaloa is what's known as a submarine volcano. This active volcano is about 3,189 feet (975 m) below sea level. Scientists estimate it'll take another 200,000 years for it to reach the surface!

The Big Island grows bigger as lava from Kilauea meets the ocean and rapidly cools and hardens.

EARTHQUAKES

So, if Hawaii doesn't sit near the meeting of two tectonic plates, how is it a **seismic** zone? Most of the archipelago's earthquakes are caused by volcanic eruptions. The ground also shakes from the weight of the islands on the Earth's crust. Others are caused by tectonic movement near fault lines. Scientists measure the strength of earthquakes using machines called seismographs.

Since most of Hawaii's earthquakes are linked to its active volcanoes, most happen around the Big Island. The state has thousands of earthquakes each year, but most are so small people don't feel them. Some, though, can cause a lot of damage, like the 1868 one on the Big Island that caused a tsunami and a landslide.

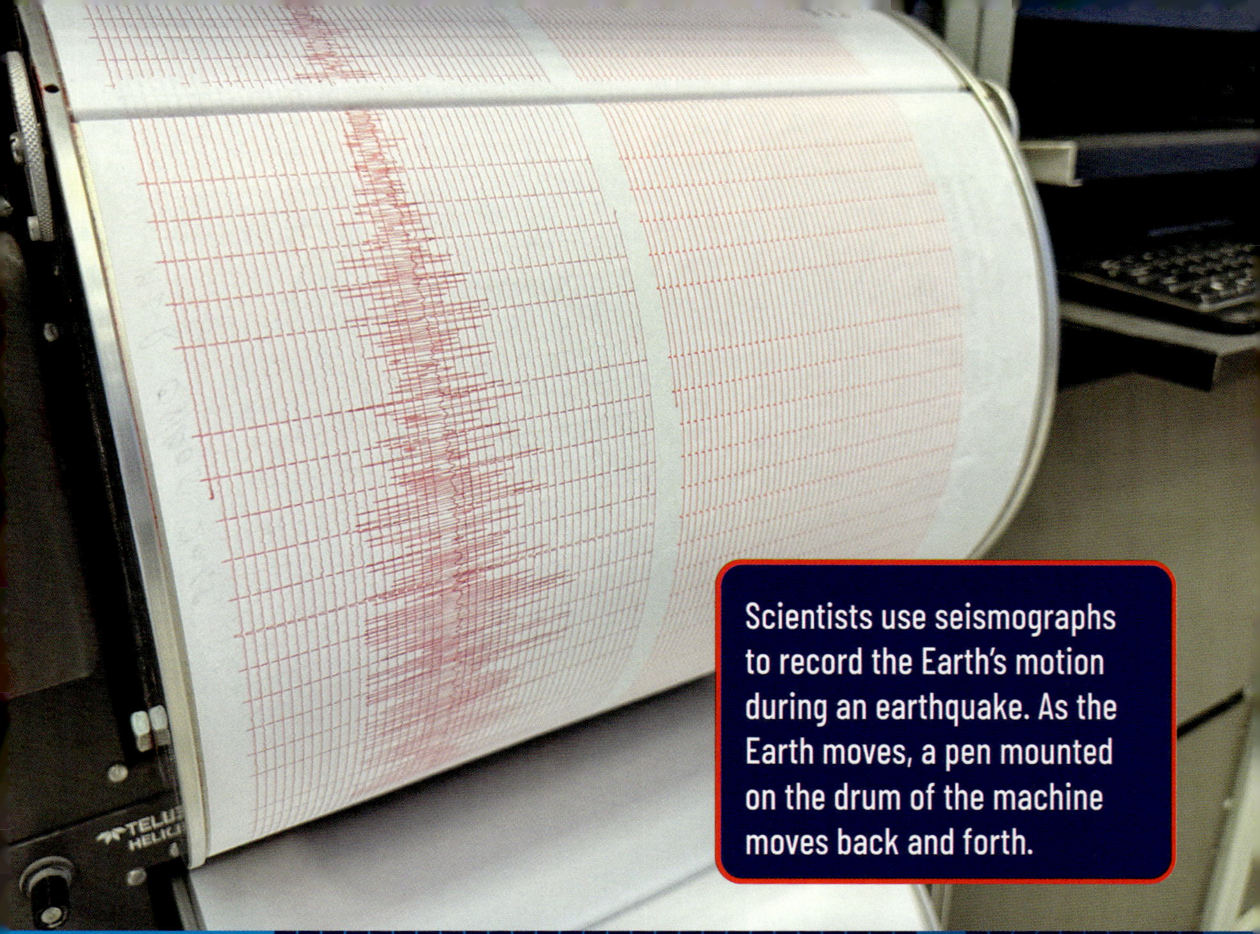

Scientists use seismographs to record the Earth's motion during an earthquake. As the Earth moves, a pen mounted on the drum of the machine moves back and forth.

EARTHQUAKE MAGNITUDES

Scientists measure the power of earthquakes using a magnitude scale. The higher the number of magnitude the stronger an earthquake is. Each point on the magnitude scale represents a 10-time increase in strength. So, a 6.5-magnitude earthquake is 10 times more powerful than a 5.5-magnitude earthquake.

There are millions of very small earthquakes—2.5 magnitude or smaller—each year. You probably don't feel them. Stronger earthquakes are rare, with only one or two over 8.0 magnitude happening each year. These earthquakes can destroy entire communities.

1868 HAWAII EARTHQUAKE

A few days before Hawaii's largest-recorded earthquake struck, Mauna Loa gave a warning signal. People on the island reported seeing a column of smoke rising out of the volcano. The next day, strong shaking began to happen, causing some damage.

During the April 2, 1868, earthquake, a stone church in Wai'ohinu collapsed.

But the big event happened April 2, 1868, when the 7.9-magnitude Ka'u earthquake struck. The quake caused landslides throughout the island and even **triggered** an eruption from Kilauea. Landslides caused mud to wash away people, homes, and livestock. Buildings collapsed and 77 people died during the disaster. To make matters worse, on April 9, a lava vent burst open on Kahuku Ranch, shooting up to 1,000 feet (300 m) into the air. The lava destroyed at least 4,000 acres (1,618 ha) of land on the ranch.

TSUNAMIS

Sometimes the most dangerous part of an earthquake and volcanic eruption is what comes after. Seismic activity can trigger a tsunami. This is a large wave that comes from the sea onto land. Most tsunamis are only about 10 feet (3 m), but some can be monstrous. The largest recorded tsunami in history was the one that hit Lituya Bay, Alaska, in 1958. It was a massive 1,700 feet (518 m) tall!

This photo shows people in Hilo, Hawaii, running from the 1946 tsunami as the waves come ashore.

Many types of earthquakes can cause tsunamis. The biggest ones are caused by earthquakes where tectonic plates meet. One such earthquake near the Aleutian Islands in Alaska—nearly 2,500 miles (4,023 km) away—triggered the worst tsunami to hit Hawaii in history in 1946. Five hours after the 7.4-magnitude quake, a tsunami that reached 55 feet (16.8 m) in height slammed into the islands.

HAWAIIAN VOLCANO OBSERVATORY

Scientists have studied the volcanoes and seismic activity in Hawaii for well over 100 years to learn more about geological processes. They can then use this knowledge to forecast eruptions elsewhere and establish safety measures.

Geologist Thomas A. Jaggar founded the HVO in 1912 to do such research. No other volcano is as active or easy to study as Kilauea, making it the perfect location to do field work. The U.S. Geological Survey (USGS), which **monitors** seismic activity across the globe, now operates the HVO. There are more than 100 stations monitoring the six volcanoes in Hawaii as well as air quality. This information allows the HVO to alert the public to dangerous conditions. This information may even lead officials to issue evacuation orders.

EARTH-SHAKING FACT!

HVO scientists have been able to use clues from Native Hawaiians' oral histories to learn more about the history of Hawaiian volcanic activity.

Technicians check one of the many volcano monitoring stations in Hawaii.

SAFETY FIRST

Thanks to organizations such as the HVO, the state of Hawaii has put many safety measures in place to protect citizens. Cities and villages use sirens to warn people of a possible tsunami. They also have evacuation routes set up to help people to safe areas if a big wave is coming.

When one of the many volcanoes is active, people in Hawaii can check air quality on a website operated by many organizations, including the USGS. The government may also issue a volcano warning and evacuation orders to people near an erupting volcano or in the path of its lava flow.

Just like the people in Florida are well prepared for a hurricane and those in the Northeast know what to do in a blizzard, the people in Hawaii know what to do when Pele decides to shake things up!

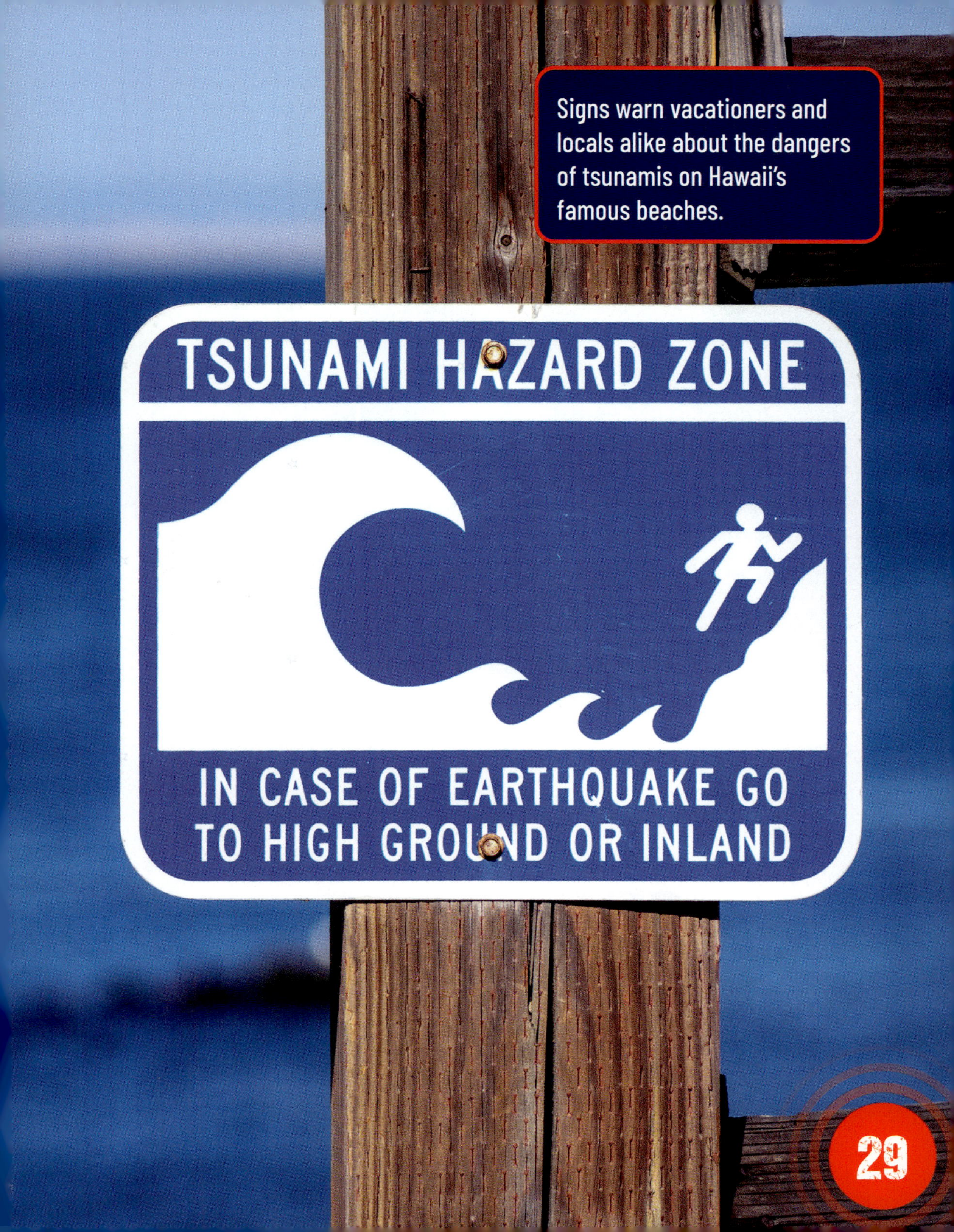

Signs warn vacationers and locals alike about the dangers of tsunamis on Hawaii's famous beaches.

GLOSSARY

airborne: Carried by the air.

culture: The beliefs and ways of life of a certain group of people.

dormant: Asleep or inactive.

emit: To send out.

geophysicist: A scientist who studies earth science.

heritage: The traditions and beliefs that are part of the history of a group or nation.

inhabited: Having people who live there.

irritate: To cause displeasure.

lava: Hot, liquid or soft rock above the surface of Earth.

magma: Hot, liquid or soft rock below the surface of Earth.

monitor: To observe and check the progress of something.

observatory: A special building for studying scientific events.

seismic: Relating to the movement of the Earth caused by an earthquake.

trigger: To cause something.

FOR MORE INFORMATION

BOOKS

Earley, Christina. *Plate Tectonics.* Coral Springs, FL: Seahorse Publishing, 2024.

Kerry, Isaac. *Tsunamis.* North Mankato, MN: Pebble, 2022.

Klepeis, Alicia. *Hawaii.* Minneapolis, MN: Bellwether Media, Inc., 2022.

WEBSITES

Britannica Kids: Tsunami
www.kids.britannica.com/kids/article/tsunami/400067
Read more about tsunamis and what causes them on the Britannica Kids website.

Hawaii Volcanoes National Park
www.nps.gov/havo/index.htm
Visit the official website of the Hawaii Volcanoes National Park.

Hawaiian Volcano Observatory
www.usgs.gov/observatories/hvo
The Hawaiian Volcano Observatory website has more information on the current conditions at the state's six volcanoes.

INDEX